PUDGIE REVOLUTION!

PIE IRON COOKIN' FOR FOOD-LOVIN' CAMPERS

JARED PIERCE · CARRIE SIMON · LIV SVANDE

PUDGIE REVOLUTION!

Pie Iron Cookin' for Food-Lovin' Campers

by Jared Pierce, Carrie Simon, Liv Svanoe

Third printing. November, 2015.

ISBN: 978-0-9890104-5-0
Rome #2009 Pudgie Revolution!

This book was funded expressly through Kickstarter support.

Published by Rome Industries, Inc.
1703 West Detweiller Drive
Peoria, IL 61615-1688
pieiron.com

TABLE OF CONTENTS

Pudgie Pie 101

What's a Pudgie Pie?

A pudgie pie is a grilled sandwich, toasted in a pie iron over a fire. Savory or sweet, quick and easy or elaborately constructed, a pudgie always satisfies. They are delicious in the great outdoors or the comfort of your own backyard. A heavenly bread pocket bursting with flavor, the pudgie pie will tickle your taste buds and satiate your soul.

A Pudgie By Any Other Name

While you may think you've never heard of a pudgie pie before, it's entirely possible you have and you just don't know it. Like a delicious international spy, the pudgie pie has many aliases. Depending on where you live or the company you keep, you may know pudgie pies as mountain pies, jaffles, camper pies, campfire pies, tonka toasters, hobo pies, toasties, or something entirely different. We've chosen to adopt the term pudgie pie because, well, that's what we've always called it.

Pudgie Pie-losophy

Everything's Better in a Pudgie
Without fail, the pie iron transforms the ordinary into the extraordinary. No matter what ingredients go in, a delectable masterpiece emerges.

A Pie Iron is All You Need
Whether you're camping, backyard cooking or stranded on a desert island, the pie iron is so versatile, it is the only tool necessary to suit all your camp-cooking needs. Teach a camper to Pudgie and she'll eat for a lifetime.

Pudgies for All
Young or old, novice cook or professional chef, pudgie pie cookery is simple and satisfying for all. Basic skills are a snap to master, but perfecting the art is a lifetime endeavor.

Creativity Reigns Supreme
What's life without risk-taking? Don't be afraid to think outside the pudgie pie box. You never know, that peanut butter and pickle pudgie might just be delicious! (see page 28)

Pudgie Pies Create Community
The pudgie pie is more than a meal; it's an experience. Nothing builds camping camaraderie more than preparing, cooking and eating pudgies together in the great outdoors.

Teach Me How to Pudgie

A pudgie pie consists of 2 basic elements: crust and filling. The crust can be any bread product or other edible pie iron-sized material and the filling is up to your wildest imagination. Whatever your choices are, you will want to follow these simple steps:

1

2

STEP 1: LOAD

Use margarine or cooking spray to thoroughly coat your iron or bread. Place one crust in the pie iron and pile on the ingredients. Keep in mind that some ingredients will cook down, so don't be afraid to make a sizeable heap. Avoid placing filling too close to the edges to avoid leaks. Beware of pointy ingredients that may threaten the integrity of your crust, place them carefully.

STEP 2: CLOSE

Either place the other crust on top of the filling, or stick it in the other side of the pie iron and close the iron with care. The key is to have some crust overhanging the edges of the iron to create a good seal. Trim excess crust with a knife.

3

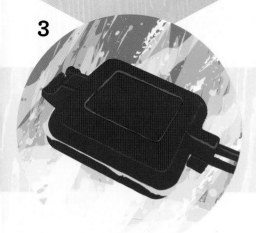

4

STEP 3: COOK

Find a good spot in the fire. A basic rule of thumb is to keep your iron as level as possible. To get a perfectly golden brown crust, peek at your pudgie's progress semi-frequently and aim for a spot in the fire over even heat. Depending on the heat level, cook your pie 3-10 minutes per side. Let the iron cool to the touch before making the next pudgie pie.

STEP 4: EAT

Remove your pudgie pie by gently flipping it out of the pie iron onto a plate. If it's stuck, use a knife to carefully loosen the edges. Then wait. It may be difficult to restrain yourself when there's a perfectly toasted pudgie pie nearby, but patience pays. Let it cool, flipping periodically, for at least 5 minutes before digging in, or run the risk of burning your mouth and compromising crucial taste buds. Fruit, berries, and tomatoes stay extra lava-hot. Always remember, pudgie safety comes first!

What a Tool! SELECTING AND CARING FOR YOUR PIE IRON

Choosing a Pie Iron: Cast Iron vs. Aluminum

A pie iron is a magical little oven that (almost) fits in your pocket. There are 2 basic pie iron types: aluminum and cast iron, and they come in a variety of shapes and sizes. While aluminum is lightweight, the pie iron is more fragile, and food is prone to burning. Cast iron is extremely durable, heats evenly, and improves with age. If we have our pudgie-druthers, we opt for the classic cast iron square for its dependability, durability and dapper good looks.

Caring for Your Cast Iron Pie Iron

Cleaning: Rinse in warm water and use a nylon brush to release any residue. Dry thoroughly. Never use soaps or detergents when cleaning your cast iron pie iron. Season your pie iron after cleaning by rubbing canola oil and sea salt in it with a paper towel. With proper care, your pie iron will create happy campers for years to come.

TIP: When the camp chair breaks and all you're left with is the bag, use it to store your pie irons. It's perfect!

The Best Thing Since Sliced Bread:
A Pie Chart of Crust Choices

There are lots of great crust options to try in your pie iron.
The sky, or your local grocery store, is the limit!

TIPS: these crusts allow for lots of space for ingredients, but keep in mind that they don't work well for particularly moist fillings; they are also very packable-they save space and won't get smashed!

TIPS: grease the iron, keep iron level while cooking

TIPS: get the largest size available; butter the bread, not the iron

JUST ADD WATER
cornbread mix
pancake mix
muffin mix

BREAD
white wheat
italian
rye potato
pumpernickel
hamburger buns
hot dog buns

FLAT/THIN
pita
flatbread
naan
spring roll wrappers
pre-cooked or fresh lasagna noodles
packaged pizza crust
flour tortillas

FROZEN AISLE
phyllo dough
puff pastry
pound cake
hashbrowns
waffles

REFRIGERATED DOUGH
crescent roll
cinnamon roll
rolled pie crust
cookie dough
biscuit
pizza

TIPS: thaw all frozen crust; keep phyllo dough covered with plastic wrap and work quickly; press hashbrowns and pound cake into greased iron

TIPS: grease the iron; stretch pizza dough to fit and press biscuit and cinnamon roll dough into iron or flatten between pieces of waxed paper; get "seamless" cresent roll dough—it's the best!; use low and slow heat when using pie crust

The Essential Pudgie Pie Dessert Box

Don't go camping without it! Nothing satisfies a sweet tooth like a dessert pudgie. Assembling a box-o-goodies is a fun and easy way to cultivate creativity and maximize dessert-liciousness. Add fresh fruit and berries to complete the package! With a proper dessert box on hand, even a pudgie novice can assemble a tasty customized masterpiece with ease. Just select any combination of ingredients that appeals to you, nestle them in the crust of your choice, and you're bound for sweet satisfaction!

Above, L to R: coconut, caramel, almonds, dried mango, pretzels, dried cranberries, pudding, pecans, cinnamon, walnuts, butterscotch chips, chocolate, toffee bits, chocolate-hazelnut spread, crystallized ginger, vanilla wafer cookies, peanut butter, marshmallows, granola, brown sugar

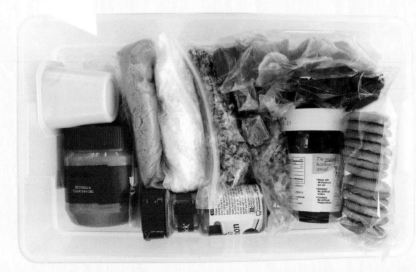

Recipe Rating Guide

● **Easy as pie.** With minimal prep
○ and ingredients, these pudgies
○ should be a snap!

● **Twice as nice.** A little extra effort
● goes a long way. While these pudgies
○ may have a few more ingredients,
or require a bit more work, the end
result is well worth the effort!

● **Pie in the sky.** Not for the faint of
● heart, these pudgies demonstrate
● a serious dedication to campfire
cooking. Go the extra mile for
supreme pudgie pleasure!

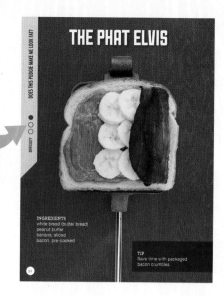

THE PHAT ELVIS

DOES THIS PUDGIE MAKE ME LOOK FAT?

DIFFICULTY ○○●

INGREDIENTS
white bread (butter bread)
peanut butter
banana, sliced
bacon, pre-cooked

TIP
Save time with packaged
bacon crumbles.

Pudgie Buddy Menu Planning

Going on a camping trip? Why wouldn't you ONLY eat pudgie pies? The
following menus contain recipes with duplicate ingredients, or as we like to
call them "Pudgie Buddies." These menus are perfect for minimizing excess
and maximizing pudgie pie consumption!

1 **Weekend Getaway:** *2 breakfasts, 2 dinners, dessert*
Morning Glory, Johnny Applekraut, Ranger Rick's Robust Reuben,
Yolkey Dokey, Dude, Where's My Caramel Apple?

2 **Gone Fishing:** *lunch, dinner, breakfast*
Friday Night Fish Fry, Taco Del Lago, Chilaquiles

3 **Daytripper:** *lunch, dinner*
Salmon Says, Gramsci

4 **On the Fly:** *3 quick entrees*
Easy as ABC, The Phat Elvis, In a PB Pickle

5 **The Sleepover:** *appetizer, dinner, dessert, breakfast*
The Great Caprese Caper, Once Upon a Lasagna, Lemon Curd is
the Word, Pardon My French Toast

C'EST La BRIE

DIFFICULTY ○ ○ ●

INGREDIENTS
puff pastry (grease iron)
brie, sliced
dried cranberries
walnuts, chopped

CRABULOUS RANGOON

DIRECTIONS

Mix equal parts cream cheese and crab meat and mix in diced carrots and scallions. Grease iron, place eggroll wrapper in iron and fill, folding toward the corner to create a triangular packet. Fold excess wrapper into the iron and repeat in other half of iron.

INGREDIENTS

eggroll wrapper (grease iron)
cream cheese
crab meat
carrots, diced
scallions, sliced

EASY as ABC

DIFFICULTY ● ○ ○

INGREDIENTS
white bread (butter bread)
cheddar cheese, sliced
apple, sliced
bacon, pre-cooked & crumbled

TIP
Save time by getting pre-cooked bacon crumbles.

FRIED GREEN TOMATO FRITTER

DIFFICULTY

DIRECTIONS
Mix equal parts panko and cornmeal and season with salt, pepper, and cayenne. Dredge green tomatoes in egg and then dry mixture. Pile into greased pie iron and cook until crisp. Serve with Sriracha mayo!

INGREDIENTS
cornmeal (grease iron)
panko
cayenne
salt/pepper
green tomatoes, 1″ cubes
egg, beaten

GETTIN' FIGGY WITH IT

DIFFICULTY ● ○ ○

INGREDIENTS
crescent roll dough (grease iron)
salami, sliced
mascarpone cheese
dried figs, sliced

DIRECTIONS
Alternate layers of salami
and mascarpone, with one
layer of figs in the middle.

recipe sponsored by Jess Osborne

GIMME SAMOSA!

● ● ○

MAKE AHEAD
Dice potatoes and carrots, boil until tender, mix with peas, onions, garlic and curry powder.

INGREDIENTS
crescent roll dough (grease iron)
potatoes, cubed
carrots, chopped
peas
onions, chopped
curry powder
garlic, minced
mango chutney

17

THE GREAT CAPRESE CAPER

DIFFICULTY ● ○ ●

INGREDIENTS
Italian bread (butter bread)
tomatoes, sliced and blotted
basil
fresh mozzarella pearls
balsamic glaze
olive tapenade

MAKE AHEAD
If you can't find pre-made balsamic glaze, simmer balsamic vinegar in a small skillet until it reduces to about 1/4 of its original volume.

TIP
Reduce the moisture content of your tomatoes by removing the liquidy center.

#HASHBROWN

DIFFICULTY

DIRECTIONS
Use 3 hashbrown patties per pudgie. Cut one patty in half and press 1 1/2 patties into buttered iron. Patch any holes with hashbrown pieces and top with ingredients.

TIP
Sear both sides over high heat, then move to a cooler spot.

INGREDIENTS
frozen hashbrown patties, thawed (grease iron)
cheddar cheese, shredded
pre-cooked sausage patty, chopped
green pepper, chopped
red pepper, chopped
red onion, chopped

BREAKFAST BURRITOMG!

DIFFICULTY

INGREDIENTS
flour tortilla (butter bread)
black beans
egg, scrambled
scallion, sliced
chorizo
cheddar cheese, shredded
salsa
avocado, cubed
sour cream
cilantro

TIPS
Use about 1 egg per pudgie
and pour over ingredients.
Keep pie iron level during first
phase of cooking.

YOLKEY DOKEY

DIRECTIONS
Make an avocado nest and carefully crack egg in center. Keep pie iron level in first cooking phase!

INGREDIENTS
English muffin bread (butter bread)
avocado, sliced
salt & pepper
egg
cheddar cheese, shredded
bacon, pre-cooked and crumbled
red onion, chopped
tomato, chopped

21

MORNING GLORY

DIFFICULTY

INGREDIENTS
grainy bread (butter bread)
carrot, shredded
zucchini, shredded and drained
pineapple, chunks
apple, chopped
brown sugar
cinnamon

INGREDIENTS (continued)
walnuts, chopped
butter
coconut, shredded

MAKE AHEAD
Mix equal parts shredded
carrot, pineapple, apple, and
shredded zucchini.

22

MUFFIN TOP

DIFFICULTY

INGREDIENTS
banana muffin mix batter
  (grease iron)
banana, sliced
chocolate chips
more muffin batter

TIPS
Fill iron as full as possible and
keep level during cooking!

CHILAQUILES

DIFFICULTY

INGREDIENTS
flour tortilla (butter bread)
egg, beaten
hot sauce
Fritos™
cheddar cheese, shredded
salsa

TIPS
Use about 1 egg per pie
and pour over ingredients.
Keep pie iron level during
first phase of cooking.

UNLEASH THE QUICHE

DIFFICULTY

DIRECTIONS
Pile veggies in pie crust. Beat
1 egg with about 2-3 Tb of
heavy cream per pie and
pour over veggies.

TIP
Keep pie iron level during first
phase of cooking.

INGREDIENTS
pie crust (grease iron)
mushrooms, sliced
kale, torn
asaigo cheese, shredded
artichoke hearts, chopped
carmelized onion
egg, beaten
heavy cream

25

PARDON my FRENCH TOAST

DIFFICULTY

INGREDIENTS
white bread (butter iron)
cream cheese
chocolate
strawberries, sliced
blueberries
pecans, chopped
egg, beaten
cinnamon
milk
vanilla

DIRECTIONS
Wisk 1 egg with 1/4 cup milk, 1/4 tsp cinnamon and 1 tsp vanilla, if desired. Dip outer side of bread in egg mixture and place in buttered pie iron. Fill with ingredients. Top with another slice of battered bread, batter side out.

JOHNNY APPLEKRAUT

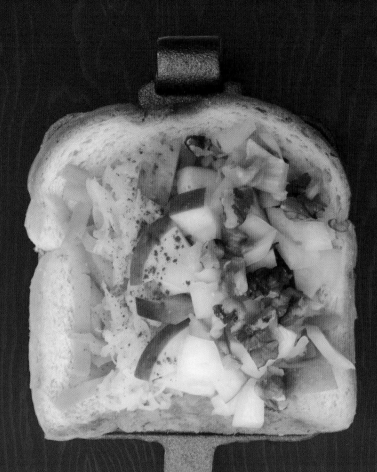

DIFFICULTY

INGREDIENTS
white bread (butter bread)
cheddar cheese, shredded
sauerkraut
apples, cubed
cinnamon
onions, diced
walnuts, chopped

27

IN A PB PICKLE

DIFFICULTY ● ○ ○

INGREDIENTS
white bread (butter bread)
peanut butter
dill pickles, sliced

TIP
Use lots of pickles!

THE CARLOS BALTHAZAR

DIFFICULTY

TIP
If you can't find guava paste in the ethnic foods aisle, a Mexican grocery store will likely have it!

recipe sponsored by Carlos Balthazar da Silveira Neto

INGREDIENTS
puff pastry, thawed
    (grease iron)
queso fresco, thickly sliced
guava paste, thickly sliced
more queso fresco,
    thickly sliced

29

LIVER-BEST

INGREDIENTS
wheat bread (butter bread)
liverwurst
cranberry mustard
red onion, sliced
Muenster cheese, sliced

DUTCH DELIGHT

DIFFICULTY

*recipe sponsored by Jasper J. Kort

INGREDIENTS
grainy bread (butter bread)
mashed potatoes
capers
kale, chopped
smoked kielbasa, sliced
gouda cheese, shredded
leeks, sliced
parsnip, sliced
parsley, chopped

31

MOO GOO GAI PIE

DIFFICULTY

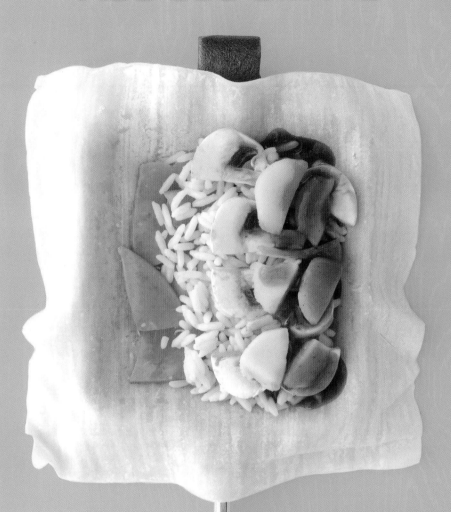

INGREDIENTS
eggroll wrapper (grease iron)
peapods, chopped
rice, pre-cooked
mushrooms, sliced
water chestnuts, chopped
stir fry sauce

TIPS
Sear over high heat, then
move to a cooler spot.
Save time by getting
packaged, pre-cooked rice.

MY GYRO!

● ○ ○ DIFFICULTY

TIP
Consider buying a gyro kit from the frozen food aisle. It has nearly everything you need!

INGREDIENTS
pita, split (butter bread)
gyro meat
tzatziki sauce
cucumber, chopped
tomatoes, chopped
onions, chopped
more gyro meat

33

PALAK PANEER PUDGIE

DIFFICULTY

INGREDIENTS
naan (butter bread)
palak paneer (or other indian spice)
   seasoning packet
heavy cream
cottage cheese, large curd
chopped frozen spinach, thawed
tomato, chopped

DIRECTIONS
Mix spice packet with
enough heavy cream to
create a paste and spread on
naan. Top with ingredients.

recipe sponsored by Tom Chelius

POUTINE DREAM

DIFFICULTY

INGREDIENTS
white bread (butter bread)
frozen waffle-cut french fries,
  thawed
gravy, pre-made
cheese curds

35

SOUTH OF THE BORDER

DIFFICULTY ● ○ ○

INGREDIENTS
whole wheat tortilla (butter bread)
black beans
mexi-corn
monteray jack cheese, shredded
pickled jalapenos
salsa verde
avocado, chopped
lime zest

recipe sponsored by Jennifer Taylor

TACO DEL LAGO

● ● ○ DIFFICULTY

DIRECTIONS
Lightly coat both sides of
fish fillet with breadcrumbs.

INGREDIENTS
flour tortilla (butter bread)
fish fillet
breadcrumbs
tartar sauce
hot sauce
Mexican blend cheese, shredded
cabbage, shredded
lime juice
cilantro

*recipe sponsored by
Lacy and Johnny Gomez*

37

THAI ONE ON

DIFFICULTY

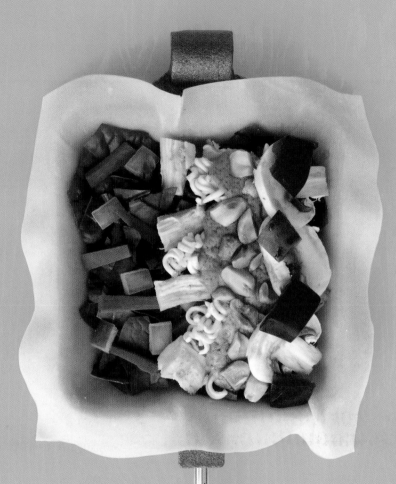

INGREDIENTS
spring roll wrappers (grease iron)
chard, chopped
carrots, chopped
red onion, chopped
cooked chicken, cubed
oriental ramen noodle seasoning
ramen noodles, pieces
peanut sauce

INGREDIENTS (continued)
peanuts, chopped
mushrooms, sliced
red pepper, chopped

TIP
Look for packaged cooked
chicken cubes in the lunchmeat
aisle to save time.

DUDE, WHERE'S MY CARAMEL APPLE?

● ○ ○

DIFFICULTY

INGREDIENTS
Texas Toast bread (butter bread)
apple, chopped
caramel sauce
peanuts, chopped

TIP
Press the interior of the bread into the pie iron to make room for lots of filling!

PBF&J

INGREDIENTS
white bread (butter bread)
peanut butter
jelly
Fritos™

PIGS in a BLANKET

● ○ ○

DIFFICULTY

INGREDIENTS
crescent roll dough (grease iron)
American cheese
mini-wieners, chopped
ketchup
more American cheese

41

PIZZA PIZZAZZ

INGREDIENTS
pizza crust, thin (butter bread)
pizza sauce
black olives, sliced
mozzarella cheese, shredded
pepperoni
onion, chopped
mushrooms, sliced

TIP
Customize with your favorite
pizza toppings!

SLOPPY JALOPY

● ●
● ●
○

INGREDIENTS
hamburger bun, large (butter bread)
meatless ground crumbles
ketchup
Worcestershire sauce
brown sugar, about 1 Tb
yellow mustard

INGREDIENTS (continued)
green pepper, chopped
onion, chopped
cheddar cheese, sliced

43

DA YOOPER

DIFFICULTY ● ● ○

INGREDIENTS
pie crust (grease iron)
potatoes, thinly sliced
cream of chicken soup
chicken, cubed
carrots, chopped
celery, chopped
onions, chopped
salt and pepper

TIP
Cook slowly over low heat.

BEER ME!

DIFFICULTY

DIRECTIONS
Soak 6 large croutons in dark beer for 5 minutes or until beer is absorbed. Place crescent roll dough in buttered iron and fill with ingredients.

INGREDIENTS
crescent roll dough (grease iron)
beer-soaked croutons
ground pepper
cheddar cheese, cubed
granny smith apple, cubed
bacon, pre-cooked
    and crumbled

recipe sponsored by Mike Brenner

KICK-A-BLEU

INGREDIENTS
white bread (butter bread)
sweet potato, thinly sliced
chicken, cubed
buffalo sauce
blue cheese, crumbled

TIPS
Cook slowly over low heat.
Look for packaged cooked
chicken cubes in the lunchmeat
aisle to save time.

FRIDAY NIGHT FISH FRY

DIFFICULTY

INGREDIENTS
marbled rye bread (butter bread)
fish fillet
tartar sauce

INGREDIENTS (continued)
lemon zest
cabbage, shredded
carrots, shredded
malt vinegar
potatoes, sliced
butter
salt/pepper, to taste

TIP
Mix the shredded cabbage
and carrots with malt vinegar
to make a coleslaw.

47

REVENGE OF THE CURDS

INGREDIENTS
wheat bread (butter bread)
broccoli, chopped
bacon, pre-cooked and crumbled
cheese curds

PACKER BACKER

DIFFICULTY

INGREDIENTS
brat bun (butter bread)
boiled beer brats, sliced in coins
sauerkraut
cheddar cheese, shredded
yellow peppers, chopped
green peppers, chopped
green onions, chopped
yellow mustard

TIP
Press bun into pie iron and patch any holes with extra bun pieces. Go Pack, Go!

49

IT'S CHILI IN HERE!

DIFFICULTY

INGREDIENTS
corn bread batter (grease iron)
chili
corn
hot sauce
sour cream
cheddar cheese, shredded
onions, chopped
more corn bread batter

TIP
One 6-oz packet of corn bread mix is enough for two pudgies.

DIRECTIONS
Prepare cornbread batter per package instructions and spread a thin layer into buttered iron, coating bottom and sides. Fill with ingredients and top with a thin layer of batter. Place on a level cooking spot over low heat. This may ooze substantially, but fear not!

50

GOBBLE IT UP!

DIFFICULTY

MAKE AHEAD
Make your own cranberry sauce
by simmering 8oz of fresh or
frozen cranberries with 1/2 cup
liquid (red wine and/or water)
with 1/4 cup sugar and 2 sprigs
fresh rosemary. Cook down to
desired consistency, ~10 min.

INGREDIENTS
potato bread (butter bread)
cranberry sauce, 2 TB
turkey cold-cuts, thickly sliced
gravy
stuffing mix

51

ONCE UPON A LASAGNA

DIFFICULTY ○ ● ●

INGREDIENTS
Italian bread (butter bread)
marinara sauce
garlic, minced
meatless ground crumbles
ricotta cheese
spinach, chopped
basil, torn
mozzarella cheese, shredded
parmesean cheese, shredded
italian herbs

TIP
Use thawed frozen spinach and remove excess water by gently squeezing in a paper towel. Mix with ricotta cheese.

LIP-SMACKIN' MAC-N-CHEESE

DIFFICULTY

TIPS
Add Sriracha for a kick or dijon mustard for mustardy-ness! Cut a piece of dough smaller than your pie iron and stretch to fit. Don't be alarmed by oozing dough!

INGREDIENTS
refrigerated pizza dough
  (grease iron)
Alfredo sauce
nutmeg
macaroni, cooked
ring bologna, bite-size pieces
smoked gouda cheese, shredded
cauliflower, chopped

53

PUDGE-YAM-A PARTY

DIFFICULTY ● ○ ○

INGREDIENTS
pie crust (grease iron)
yams, thinly sliced
cinnamon
marshmallows
brown sugar
pecans, chopped

TIP
Cook slowly over low heat.

PORKIE PUDGIE

DIFFICULTY

INGREDIENTS
Hawaiian roll (butter bread)
Muenster cheese, sliced
BBQ pulled pork
red onion, chopped
cabbage, shredded
spicy relish

TIP
Slow roast your own BBQ pork
if you're feeling ambitious!

55

TATER TOT™ CASSEROLE

INGREDIENTS
frozen hashbrown patties, thawed
  (grease iron)
cream of mushroom soup
meatless ground crumbles
mushrooms, sliced
cheddar cheese, shredded
frozen french-cut green beans,
  thawed
French fried onions

DIRECTIONS
Use 3 hashbrown patties per
pudgie. Cut one patty in half and
press 1 1/2 patties into buttered
pie iron. Patch holes with hashbrown pieces; top with ingredients.

TIP
Sear both sides over high heat,
then move to a cooler spot.

THE GREAT PUMPKIN PIE

DIFFICULTY

INGREDIENTS
pie crust (grease iron)
cream cheese
vanilla wafer cookie pieces
pumpkin butter
pecans, chopped
more vanilla wafer
   cookie pieces

57

TUNA CASSEROLE

DIFFICULTY ● ○ ○

INGREDIENTS
white bread (butter bread)
cheddar cheese, sliced
cream of mushroom soup
egg noodles, uncooked
celery, sliced
onion, chopped
tuna
ground pepper

TIP
Nestle noodles in soup and
cook slowly over low heat.

COME KALE AWAY

DIFFICULTY

MAKE AHEAD
Halve butternut squash and
remove seeds. Drizzle with
olive oil, salt and pepper.
Bake in a 350 degree oven
for 30 minutes or until fork-
tender. Let cool and mash.

INGREDIENTS
flatbread (butter bread)
roasted butternut squash mash
apple chicken sausage, sliced
Muenster cheese, sliced
cranberry sauce
kale, chopped

59

GO FOR THE GOLDMYER!

INGREDIENTS
ciabatta bread (butter bread)
peppered turkey, sliced
dill havarti cheese, sliced
avocado, sliced
jalapeño mayonnaise
kalamata olives, sliced
red peppers, chopped
red onion, chopped

DIRECTIONS
Dice jalapeños, removing seeds and membranes to tone down the heat. Mix with mayonnaise.

CURRY UP and WAIT

INGREDIENTS
crescent roll dough (grease iron)
red curry paste
fresh ginger, minced
kabocha squash, sliced
unsweetened coconut milk
  solids
lime zest
peanuts, chopped
cilantro

A REAL FUNGI

DIFFICULTY ● ● ●

INGREDIENTS
Italian bread (butter bread)
Alfredo sauce
spinach, chopped
shallots, chopped
garlic, minced
mixed mushrooms, chopped
balsamic redux
asiago cheese, shredded
bacon, pre-cooked
  and crumbled

MAKE-AHEAD
Prepare a balsamic redux
by boiling balsamic vinegar
until it reduces in volume
by ¾.

SALMON SAYS

DIFFICULTY ● ○ ○

TIP
Patch any perforation holes in the crust with pieces of pita bread.

INGREDIENTS
pita, split (butter bread)
smoked salmon
cream cheese
pesto

*recipe sponsored by Kent Carter

63

PUFF the MAGIC PUDGIE

DIFFICULTY ● ● ●

INGREDIENTS
puff pastry (grease iron)
artichoke spread
garlic, minced
mushrooms, sliced
roasted red pepper, chopped
asiago, shredded

TIPS
Roast a red pepper over the campfire by holding it in the flame until the skin is charred black. Use a paper towel to rub off the black skin, chop and enjoy!

Fill sparingly to give puff pastry room to expand.

64

BEST-O-PESTO

DIFFICULTY

INGREDIENTS
wheat wrap (butter bread)
pesto
cooked chicken, chopped
red pepper, chopped
garlic, minced
red onion, chopped
mozzarella cheese, shredded

TIP
Look for packaged cooked
chicken cubes in the lunchmeat aisle to save time.

65

SQUASH YOUR HUNGER

DIFFICULTY ● ● ○

INGREDIENTS
spinach wrap (butter bread)
roasted butternut squash mash
asparagus, sliced
sausage
roasted garlic
gorgonzola cheese
walnuts, chopped

MAKE AHEAD
Halve butternut squash and remove seeds. Drizzle with olive oil, salt and pepper. Bake in a 350 degree oven for 30 minutes or until fork-tender. Let cool and mash.

THE HOOPER

● ○ ○ DIFFICULTY

INGREDIENTS
crescent roll dough (grease iron)
arugula, torn
dried figs, chopped
goat cheese, crumbled
pear, sliced
walnuts, chopped

TIP
Use goat cheese sparingly.

*recipe sponsored by Pinto Bella Hoops

CHICAGO-STYLE HOTDOGGIN'

INGREDIENTS
hot dog bun, split (butter bread)
hot dog, sliced
celery salt
pickle relish, sweet
hot peppers
sport peppers, sliced
pickle spear, sliced
onion, diced

INGREDIENTS (continued)
tomato, diced
yellow mustard
poppy seeds

TIPS
Use plenty of celery salt!
Sprinkle poppy seeds on
outside of buttered bun for a
DIY poppyseed bun.

DOUBLE D RANCH

DIFFICULTY

TIP
Look for packaged cooked chicken cubes in the lunchmeat aisle to save time.

INGREDIENTS
Texas Toast bread (butter bread)
cooked chicken, cubed
ranch dressing
bacon, pre-cooked
pepperjack cheese, sliced
green chiles, canned
red pepper, chopped
tomato, chopped
scallions, sliced

recipe sponsored by Doug and Dennise Pierce

69

GRAMSCI

DIFFICULTY ● ○ ○

INGREDIENTS
pita bread, split (butter bread)
salami, sliced
string cheese, sliced
pepperoni, sliced
mayonnaise
pickled red pepper
dijon mustard

TIPS
Pickle your own red pepper
by soaking chopped red
pepper in vinegar and salt.
Patch any perforation holes
in the crust with pieces of
pita bread.

PICKLE PATTY PUDGIE on PUMPERNICKEL

● ● ○ DIFFICULTY

DIRECTIONS

Gently mix ground beef with a dash of Worcestershire, salt and pepper. Spread raw beef mixture on bread and top with ingredients. Include lots of pickles!

INGREDIENTS

pumpernickel bread (butter bread)
ground beef, lean
salt & pepper
Worcestershire sauce
ketchup
yellow mustard
onions, chopped
pickles
cheddar cheese, sliced

RANGER RICK'S ROBUST REUBEN

DIFFICULTY ● ○ ○

INGREDIENTS
pumpernickel bread (butter bread)
corned beef, sliced
swiss cheese, sliced
spicy horseradish sauce
sauerkraut
more corned beef, sliced

DIRECTIONS
To make spicy horseradish sauce, mix sour cream, horseradish, and Sriracha to taste.

recipe sponsored by Rick Bergman

SEÑOR HOT DOG

DIFFICULTY

MAKE AHEAD
Slice white onion and
sauté over medium heat
until browned.

INGREDIENTS
hot dog bun (butter bread)
hot dog, sliced
fried onions
mayonnaise
Sriracha
guacamole
bacon, pre-cooked
  and crumbled

recipe sponsored by Atlee and Julie Svanoe

73

DIFFICULTY ● ● ○

THE AUNTIE MARY

INGREDIENTS
large Kaiser roll, split (butter bread)
muffaletta spread
mortadella, sliced
capicola, sliced
sweet peppers, sliced
ham, sliced
salami, sliced
more muffaletta spread
provolone cheese

TIP
Butter outside of split roll
and press interior of roll
into pie iron.

recipe sponsored by Joe Gullo

WIN ME DOVER

● ○ ○

DIFFICULTY

TIP
Plug the bagel hole with a
piece of turkey or bagel!

*recipe sponsored by Erik Evensen
and Erika Svanoe*

INGREDIENTS
thin bagels (butter bread)
turkey, sliced
Sriracha, to taste
cheddar cheese, sliced
hummus
sun-dried tomatoes, chopped

PHILLY CHEESE STEAK-OUT

DIFFICULTY ● ○ ○

INGREDIENTS
white bread (butter bread)
beef, cooked & sliced
onion, diced
brick cheese, sliced
mushrooms, sliced

TIP
Look for pre-cooked sliced
steak in the freezer or
refrigerator aisle.

SUBLIME LIME

● ●
● ○

DIFFICULTY

TIP
Use about 3/4 of a pudding
cup per pudgie pie.

*recipe sponsored by
Jeanne and Larry Meile*

INGREDIENTS
pie crust (grease iron)
vanilla wafer cookie pieces
tapioca pudding
lime zest
coconut, shredded
lime, sliced, rind removed
sugar, 1 tsp
more vanilla wafer
   cookie pieces

77

APPLE of my PIE

DIFFICULTY

INGREDIENTS
crescent roll dough (grease iron)
cream cheese
cinnamon
honey
apples, chopped
raisins
walnuts, chopped

recipe sponsored by Kim Elder

BERRY CINN-FUL

DIFFICULTY

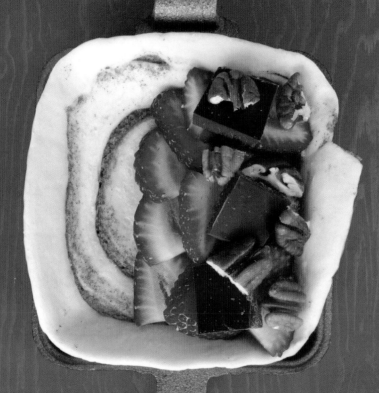

TIPS
Flatten cinnamon roll dough between sheets of waxed paper. Cinnamon bread works great, too!

INGREDIENTS
cinnamon roll dough, large (grease iron)
strawberries, sliced
dark chocolate, pieces
pecans, chopped

recipe sponsored by Loni E. Davis

DREAMY BANANA CREAM

INGREDIENTS
white bread (butter bread)
banana, sliced
vanilla yogurt
granola
marshmallows
brown sugar
coconut

GROW A PEAR

DIFFICULTY

INGREDIENTS
puff pastry (grease iron)
homegrown pears, sliced
honey, 1 TB
pistachios
almonds, chopped
dried cherries, chopped
almond paste, broken into
    small chunks

TIP
Easy on the almond paste
(1TB), heavy on the pears.

81

LEGGO MY MANGO

DIFFICULTY

INGREDIENTS
brownie crust (grease iron)
mango, sliced
sea salt
coconut
chocolate covered pomegranate bits
pistachios, chopped

MAKE AHEAD
Prepare a box brownie batter, but bake it in 2 pans (adjust baking time) to create 1/2 inch brownies. Cool in pan, cut pieces to pie iron size, and layer between waxed paper for transport.

LEMON CURD IS THE WORD

DIFFICULTY

INGREDIENTS
white bread (butter bread)
lemon curd, 2 TB
blueberries
basil, torn
pine nuts
vanilla wafer cookie pieces

TIP
Lemon curd packs a punch!
Be careful not to over-do it.

83

PEACHY KEEN

DIFFICULTY

INGREDIENTS
pound cake, sliced (grease iron)
chocolate-hazelnut spread
peaches, sliced
blueberries
crystallized ginger, chopped

DIRECTIONS
Cut 4 1/2-inch slices of
pound cake. Lay 2 slices into
buttered pie iron and press
down. Fill with ingredients.
Press the remaining 2 slices
into the other buttered side
of the pie iron and close.

RHUBARBARIAN

TIPS
Place a few pie crust scraps in the middle of the pie to absorb excess moisture. Cook slowly over low heat.

INGREDIENTS
pie crust (grease iron)
rhubarb, thinly sliced
crystallized ginger, chopped
pie crust scraps
strawberries, sliced
lemon zest
sugar, about 1TB
more rhubarb, thinly sliced

ROSEMARY'S PUDGIE

DIFFICULTY

INGREDIENTS
brownie (grease iron)
raspberries
fresh rosemary, chopped
hazelnuts, chopped

MAKE AHEAD
Prepare a box brownie batter,
but bake it in 2 pans (adjust
baking time) to create 1/2
inch brownies. Cool in pan,
cut pieces to pie iron size,
and layer between waxed
paper for transport.

TOFFEE BREAK

TIP
Use about half of a pudding
cup per pudgie pie.

INGREDIENTS
white bread (butter bread)
toffee bits
vanilla pudding
coffee powder, 1 TB
chocolate, pieces
almonds, sliced

ALMOND JOYOUS

DIFFICULTY ● ○ ○

INGREDIENTS
white bread (butter bread)
dark chocolate, pieces
coconut
almonds, chopped
dried cranberries

88

BAKLA-VA-VA-VOOM!

●●
●●●
●●

DIFFICULTY

DIRECTIONS
Use 5 sheets of phyllo dough
for the outer layers and 2
sheets for each inner layer.
Fill each layer with nuts, spices,
butter and lots of honey.

INGREDIENTS
phyllo dough (grease iron)
walnuts, finely chopped
pistachios, finely chopped
honey
cinnamon
nutmeg
cardamom
butter

89

CANDY is DANDY

INGREDIENTS
white bread (butter bread)
Snickers™, sliced
banana, sliced
peanut butter cups, chopped

SO, A PUDGIE WALKS INTO A BAR...

TIP
Pack your sweetened condensed milk in a squeeze bottle for convenient use and storage!

INGREDIENTS
pie crust (grease iron)
pretzels, broken
chocolate, pieces
coconut
pecans, chopped
toffee bits
sweetened condensed milk

THE PHAT ELVIS

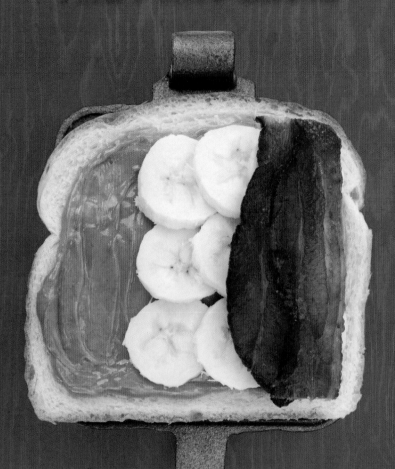

INGREDIENTS
white bread (butter bread)
peanut butter
banana, sliced
bacon, pre-cooked

TIP
Save time with packaged
bacon crumbles.

92

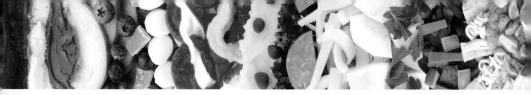

ACKNOWLEDGEMENTS

First and foremost, tremendous thanks to Erik Evensen, who used his magical powers of design and many hours of his free time to make this book look better than we ever could have imagined.

Thanks to our generous Kickstarter backers for turning our pudgie pie cookbook dreams into a reality and for staying patient while that metamorphosis took longer than anticipated.

Thanks to Bill and Jess Osborne for being people of action and prompting opportunity to come knocking on our door.

Thanks to Michael O'Russa for sharing our passion for pudgie pies and being instrumental in helping to spread the pudgie love near and far.

Thanks to Daniel Kinney who so generously donated his time, love of rhubarb, and audio-visual expertise. Somehow he managed to make us look like we knew what we were doing.

Thanks to our faithful pudgie pals who enthusiastically taste-tested copious incarnations of recipes and offered valuable feedback, even when they couldn't possibly eat another bite.

Thanks to all the family and friends who have influenced our love of cooking, camping, and eating good food.

Finally, thanks to everyone who ever ate a pudgie pie with us and said, "You guys should write a cookbook!" We couldn't have done it without you.

THE COMPLETE PUDGIE PIE INDEX

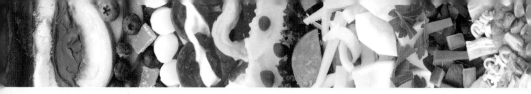

CRUST INDEX

ABOUT THE AUTHORS

Liv Svanoe would rather be cooking. She started making pudgie pies as a young Girl Scout and it was love at first taste. She has been honing her skills of pudgery ever since. A devoted pudgie pioneer, she won't rest until happy campers everywhere have discovered the joy of pudgery. She loves to camp, kayak, and create new and exciting campfire cuisine.

Carrie Simon would rather be camping. She sleeps in a tent as often as she can and it's never enough. At home, she grows vegetables and turns them into creative culinary concoctions. Self-proclaimed foodie and burgeoning locavore, there's no place she'd rather be cooking than in the great outdoors. These two loves collide in the pudgie pie!

Jared Pierce would rather be eating. He gets hungry traversing the Wisconsin wilderness and nothing satisfies him more than a piping hot pudgie straight off the press. He comes from a long line of avid outdoorsmen and eating enthusiasts, and has spent years perfecting his campfire cooking expertise.